A GARDEN OF INSPIRATION

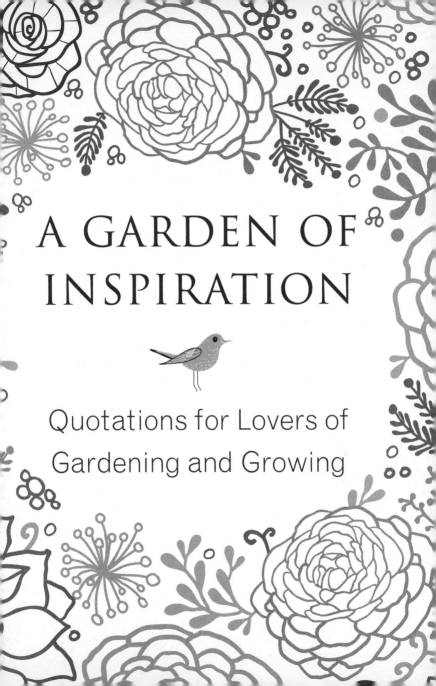

A GARDEN OF INSPIRATION

Quotations for Lovers of Gardening and Growing

A Garden of Inspiration

Text copyright © 2015 Hatherleigh Press

Library of Congress Cataloging-in-Publication Data is available upon request.

ISBN: 978-1-57826-554-1

Cover and Interior Design by Carolyn Kasper

Printed in the United States

10 9 8 7 6 5 4 3 2 1

Contents

Introduction

OU SENSE it the first time your hands sink into the earth and the aroma of fresh soil fills the air. The feeling deepens when the first flower emerges and the first vegetable is plucked from the vine. Before long you are plotting additional beds, searching for new variations to plant, nurturing each new addition like a proud parent. The world around you seems new. The changing climates and seasons hold more significance.

You are bonded with nature. You are giving back something to the Earth you live on, making it more beautiful and replenishing it with new growth.

Soon, you find yourself wandering to the garden for no particular reason. Suddenly it has become a haven for you when you need healing. It is here that you discover that more than plants are cultivated in a garden. The gardener also grows. Your breathing slows and your mind relaxes with every movement of the hoe and trowel. Sweat and soul collide in the garden... with growth as its result.

That is when you know it. You are a gardener.

We invite you now to take a relaxing stroll through the pages of *A Garden of Inspiration*. Let these words speak to your gardener's heart and inspire your love of nature, as we celebrate the true spirit of gardening!

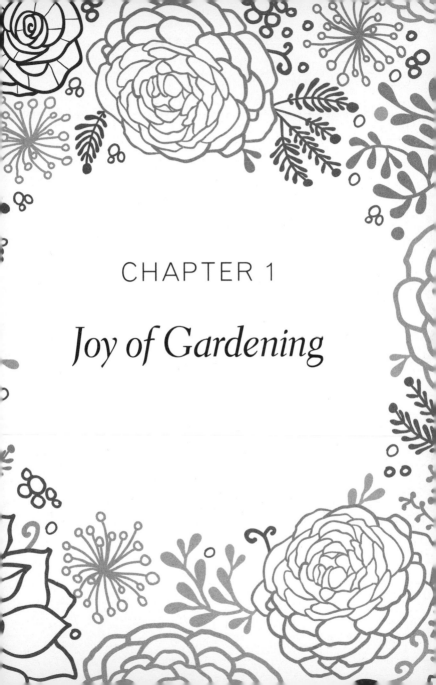

CHAPTER 1

Joy of Gardening

WHEN I go into the garden with a spade, and dig a bed, I feel such an exhilaration and health that I discover that I have been defrauding myself all this time in letting others do for me what I should have done with my own hands.

—RALPH WALDO EMERSON

There is peace in the garden. Peace and results.

—RUTH STOUT

There are many tired gardeners, but I've seldom met old gardeners. I know many elderly gardeners but the majority are young at heart. Gardening simply does not allow one to be mentally old, because too many hopes and dreams are yet to be realized. The one absolute of gardeners is faith. Regardless of how bad past gardens have been, every gardener believes that next year's will be better. It is easy to age when there is nothing to believe in, nothing to hope for, gardeners, however, simply refuse to grow up.

—ALLAN ARMITAGE

The glory of gardening: hands in the dirt, head in the sun, heart with nature. To nurture a garden is to feed not just on the body, but the soul.

—ALFRED AUSTIN

No sooner did I bend over and scratch the soil with the hoe that I began to unearth bits and pieces of my past. Memories forever rooted in time were clustered in my garden consciousness like potatoes, waiting, crying to be dug up....I plant flowers and vegetables. I harvest memories—and life.

—NANCY H. JORDAN

So, yes, I do experience a type of reverie as a gardener. But it is not something I control or strive for. When I find spirituality in my garden, it seems to go hand in hand with hard work and diligence. Like a burst of sunshine on a cloudy day, a feeling of peace will come over me and grab me by surprise. I don't really know why or how it happens. But then again, I wouldn't want it any other way.

—FRAN SORIN

Gardening is a metaphor for life, teaching you to nourish new life and weed out that which cannot succeed.

—NELSON MANDELA

Garden making, like gardening itself, concerns the relationship of the human being to his natural surroundings.

—RUSSELL PAGE

No occupation is so delightful to me as the culture of the earth, no culture comparable to that of the garden...But though an old man, I am but a young gardener.

—THOMAS JEFFERSON

An hour's hard digging is a good way of getting one's mind back in the right perspective.

—RICHARD BRIERS

It was a perfect day
For sowing...
Nothing undone
Remained; the early seeds
All safely sown.

And now, hark at the rain,
Windless and light,
Half a kiss, half a tear,
Saying good-night.

—Edward Thomas, "Sowing"

In almost every garden, the land is made better and so is the gardener.

—Robert Rodale

The great challenge for the garden designer is not to make the garden look natural, but to make the garden so that the people in it will feel natural.

—Lawrence Halprin

A garden is not a place: it is a passage, a passion. We don't know where we're going; to pass through is enough; to pass through is to remain.

—Octavio Paz

A garden is a reflection of its owner, a thing of beauty that changes over time, a window to the creativity within.

—LEE MILLER

To create a garden is to search for a better world. In our effort to improve on nature, we are guided by a vision of paradise. Whether the result is a horticultural masterpiece or only a modest vegetable patch, it is based on the expectation of a glorious future. This hope for the future is at the heart of all gardening.

—MARINA SCHINZ

There is peace within a garden,
    a peace so deep and calm,
That when the heart is troubled,
    it's like a soothing balm.
There's life within a garden,
    a life that still goes on,

Filling the empty places when older
    plants have gone.
There's glory in the garden at every
    time of year.
Spring, summer, autumn, winter,
    to fill the heart with cheer.
So ever tend your garden, its beauty
    to increase.
For in it you'll find solace. And in it
    you'll find peace.

—LADY ROSAMUND LANGHAM

We gardeners are healthy, joyous, natural creatures. We are practical, patient, optimistic. We declare our optimism every year, every season, with every act of planting.

—CAROL DEPPE,
    The Resilient Gardener:
    Food Production and
    Self-reliance in Uncertain
    Times

To garden, you open your personal space to admit a few, a great many, or thousands of plants which exude charm, pleasure, beauty, oxygen, conversation, friendship, confidence, and other rewards should you succeed in meeting their basic needs. This is why people garden. It can be easy but challenging, and the rewards are priceless.

—TOM CLOTHIER

Everything that slows us down and forces patience, everything that sets us back into the slow circles of nature is a help. Gardening is an instrument of grace.

—MAY SARTON

A gardener learns more in the mistakes than in the successes.

—BARBARA DODGE BORLAND

What continues to astonish me about a garden is that you can walk past it in a hurry, see something wrong, stop to set it right, and emerge an hour or two later breathless, contented, and wondering what on earth happened.

—DOROTHY GILMAN

The most noteworthy thing about gardeners is that they are always optimistic, always enterprising, and never satisfied. They always look forward to doing something better than they have ever done before.

—VITA SACKVILLE-WEST

People are turning to their gardens not to consume but to actively create, not to escape from reality but to observe it closely. In doing this they experience the connectedness of creation and the profoundest sources of being. That the world we live in and the activity of making it are one seamless whole is something that we may occasionally glimpse. In the garden, we know.

—CAROL WILLIAMS,
Bringing a Garden to Life

The greatest gift of the garden is the restoration of the five senses.

—HANNA RION

But gardening is none of that, really. Strip away the gadgets and the techniques, the books and the magazines and the soil test kits, and what you're left with, at the end of the day, is this: a stretch of freshly turned dirt, a handful of seeds scratched into the surface, and a marker to remember where they went. It is at the same time an incredibly brave and an incredibly simple thing to do, entrusting your seeds to the earth and waiting for them to rise up out of the ground to meet you.

—AMY STEWART,
*From the Ground Up: The
Story of a First Garden*

Gardeners must dance with feedback, play with results, turn as they learn. Learning to think as a gardener is inseparable from the acts of gardening. Learning how to garden is learning how to slow down. Wise is the person whose heart and mind listen to what Nature says. Time will tell, but we often fail to listen.

—MICHAEL P. GAROFALO,
Pulling Onions

Today I think
Only with scents,—scents dead
    leaves yield,
And bracken, and wild carrot's seed,
And the square mustard field...
It is enough
To smell, to crumble the dark
    earth...

—EDWARD THOMAS, "Digging"

He talked and contrived endlessly to the effect that I should understand the land, not as a commodity, an inert fact to be taken for granted, but as an ultimate value, enduring and alive, useful and beautiful and mysterious and formidable and comforting, beneficent and terribly demanding, worthy of the best of a man's attention and care… he insisted that I learn to do the hard labor that the land required, knowing—and saying again and again—that the ability to do such work is the source of a confidence and an independence of character that can come no other way, not by money, not by education.

—WENDELL BERRY,
The Hidden Wound

My spirit was lifted and my soul nourished by my time in the garden. It gave me a calm connection with all of life, and an awareness that remains with me now, long after leaving the garden.

—NANCY ROSS

Whoever makes a garden
Has oh so many friends:
The glory of the morning,

The dew when daylight ends,
And rain and wind and sunshine
And dew and fertile sod,
For he who makes a garden
Works hand in hand with God.

—Author Unknown

If you've never experienced the joy of accomplishing more than you can imagine, plant a garden.

—Robert Brault

God Almighty first planted a Garden. And indeed it is the purest of human pleasures. It is the greatest refreshment to the spirits of man, without which buildings and palaces are but gross handiworks. And a man shall ever see, that when ages grow to civility and elegancy, men come to build stately sooner than to garden finely, as if gardening were the greater perfection.

—Sir Francis Bacon

There is no gardening without humility. Nature is constantly sending even its oldest scholars to the bottom of the class for some egregious blunder.

—Alfred Austin

At the heart of gardening there is a belief in the miraculous.

—Mirabel Osler

People who spend a great deal of time in their gardens attest to the natural mindfulness that gardening requires. What could be more naturally mindful than weeding? It requires a great deal of sustained attention. Weeds need to be taken up with care: pull too hard, and the weed breaks in your fingers, leaving the root to grow and spread. Different weeds need different techniques and, sometimes, tools. When we weed our gardens, we have to pay attention to where and how we walk and bend. Move too far in one direction or another, and we'll squash growing things.

—SURA LAMA DAS

Half the interest of a garden is the constant exercise of the imagination. You are always living three, or indeed six, months hence. I believe that people entirely devoid of imagination never can be really good gardeners. To be content with the present, and not striving about the future, is fatal.

—ALICE MORSE EARLE

Let no one think that real gardening is a bucolic and meditative occupation. It is an insatiable passion, like everything else to which a man gives his heart.

—KAREL ČAPEK,
The Gardener's Year

Whoever makes a garden
Has never worked alone;
The rain has always found it,
The sun has always known;
The wind has blown across it
And helped to scatter seeds;
Whoever makes a garden
Has all the help he needs.

—Author Unknown

A garden is a grand teacher. It teaches patience and careful watchfulness; it teaches industry and thrift; above all it teaches entire trust.

—Gertrude Jekyll

When the world wearies and society fails to satisfy, there is always the garden.

—Minnie Aumonier

The garden, historically, is the place where all the senses are exploited. Not just the eye, but the ear—with water, with birds. And there is texture, too, in plants you long to touch.

—WILLIAM HOWARD ADAMS

A garden should make you feel you've entered privileged space—a place not just set apart but reverberant—and it seems to me that, to achieve this, the gardener must put some kind of twist on the existing landscape, turn its prose into something nearer poetry.

—MICHAEL POLLAN

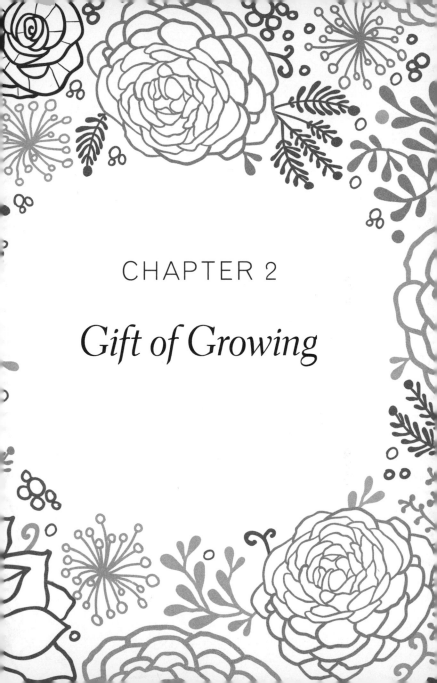

CHAPTER 2

Gift of Growing

DD AS I am sure it will appear to some, I can think of no better form of personal involvement in the cure of the environment than that of gardening. A person who is growing a garden, if he is growing it organically, is improving a piece of the world. He is producing something to eat, which makes him somewhat independent of the grocery business, but he is also enlarging, for himself, the meaning of food and the pleasure of eating.

—WENDELL BERRY, *The Art of the Commonplace: The Agrarian Essays*

The work of a garden bears visible fruits—
in a world where most of our labors seem
suspiciously meaningless.

—PAM BROWN

With rake and seeds and sower,
And hoe and line and reel,
When the meadows shrill with
    "peeping"
And the old world wakes from
    sleeping,
Who wouldn't be a grower
That has any heart to feel?

—FREDERICK FRYE ROCKWELL,
    "Invitation," *Around the
    Year in the Garden*

Any garden demands as much of its maker
as he has to give. But I do not need to tell
you, if you are a gardener, that no other
undertaking will give as great a return for
the amount of effort put into it.

—ELIZABETH LAURENCE

I grow plants for many reasons: to please my soul, to challenge the elements or to challenge my patience, for novelty, or for nostalgia, but mostly for the joy in seeing them grow.

—DAVID HOBSON

When all is said and done, is there any more wonderful sight, any moment when man's reason is nearer to some sort of contact with the nature of the world than the sowing of seeds, the planting of cuttings, the transplanting of shrubs or the grafting of slips.

—ST. AUGUSTINE

The first gatherings of the garden in May of salads, radishes and herbs made me feel like a mother about her baby—how could anything so beautiful be mine. And this emotion of wonder filled me for each vegetable as it was gathered every year.

There is nothing that is comparable to it, as satisfactory or as thrilling, as gathering the vegetables one has grown.

—Alice B. Toklas

When the sun rises, I go to work.
When the sun goes down I take
    my rest,
I dig the well from which I drink,
I farm the soil which yields my food,
I share creation, Kings can do
    no more.

— Chinese Proverb

Every plant teaches us. When the blossom dies, the fruit appears in it.

—Vikrant Parsai

All gardeners need to know when to accept something wonderful and unexpected, taking no credit except for letting it be.

—Allen Lacy

A garden requires patient labor and attention. Plants do not grow merely to satisfy ambitions or to fulfill good intentions. They thrive because someone expended effort on them.

—LIBERTY HYDE BAILEY

He who works his land will have abundant food.

—PROVERBS 12:11

Of all the wonderful things in the wonderful universe of God, nothing seems to me more surprising than the planting of a seed in the blank earth and the result thereof.

—JULIE MOIR MESSERVY

Yes, in the poor man's garden grow
Far more than herbs and flowers—
Kind thoughts, contentment, peace
    of mind,
And joy for weary hours.

—MARY HOWITT

Though I do not believe that a plant will spring up where no seed has been, I have great faith in a seed. Convince me that you have a seed there, and I am prepared to expect wonders.

—HENRY DAVID THOREAU

The purpose of agriculture is not the production of food, but the perfection of human beings.

—MASANOBU FUKUOKA

Most of all, one discovers that the soil does not stay the same, but, like anything alive, is always changing and telling its own story. Soil is the substance of transformation.

—CAROL WILLIAMS

A garden is evidence of faith. It links us with all the misty figures of the past who also planted and were nourished by the fruits of their planting.

—GLADYS TABER

Man—despite his artistic pretensions, his sophistication, and his many accomplishments—owes his existence to a six inch layer of topsoil and the fact that it rains.

—Author Unknown

The glory of gardening: hands in the dirt, head in the sun, heart with nature. To nurture a garden is to feed not just on the body, but the soul.

—Alfred Austin

The earth is absolutely honest; it gives back what is put into it plus interest on the time, money and effort invested. Treat soil handsomely and it will give you a rich return.

—Patience Strong

A society grows great when old men plant trees whose shade they know they shall never sit in.

—Greek Proverb

To forget how to dig the earth and to tend the soil is to forget ourselves.

—MAHATMA GANDHI

The single greatest lesson the garden teaches is that our relationship to the planet need not be zero-sum, and that as long as the sun still shines and people still can plan and plant, think and do, we can, if we bother to try, find ways to provide for ourselves without diminishing the world.

—MICHAEL POLLAN,
*The Omnivore's Dilemma:
A Natural History of Four
Meals*

Removing the weeds, putting fresh soil about the bean stems, and encouraging this weed which I had sown, making the yellow soil express its summer thought in bean leaves and blossoms, rather than in wormwood and piper and millet grass, making the earth say beans instead of grass—this was my daily work...

> —HENRY DAVID THOREAU,
> *Walden (Or Life in the Woods)*

I believe that virtually everyone has the ability to either grow some food at home, or to find an appropriate location to start a garden. I may sound like a kook who plants my landscape with cucumbers instead of carnations, peppers instead of petunias, and fruit trees rather than ficus, but I am convinced that wherever you go, you can grow food! Now is the time for us to join together and plant the seeds that will transform the places in which we live.

> —GREG PETERSON,
> *Grow Wherever You Go! Discovering the Place Where Your Garden Lives*

I have found, through years of practice, that people garden in order to make something grow; to interact with nature; to share, to find sanctuary, to heal, to honor the earth, to leave a mark. Through gardening, we feel whole as we make our personal work of art upon our land.

—Julie Moir Messervy,
The Inward Garden

I used to visit and revisit it a dozen times a day, and stand in deep contemplation over my vegetable progeny with a love that nobody could share or conceive of who had never taken part in the process of creation. It was one of the most bewitching sights in the world to observe a hill of beans thrusting aside the soil, or a rose of early peas just peeping forth sufficiently to trace a line of delicate green.

—Nathaniel Hawthorne,
Mosses from an Old Manse

The foolish man seeks happiness in the distance, the wise grows it under his feet.

—JAMES OPPENHEIM

Ripe vegetables were magic to me. Unharvested, the garden bristled with possibility. I would quicken at the sight of a ripe tomato, sounding its redness from deep amidst the undifferentiated green. To lift a bean plant's hood of heart shaped leaves and discover a clutch of long slender pods handing underneath could make me catch my breath.

—MICHAEL POLLAN

"Green fingers" are a fact, and a mystery only to the unpracticed. But green fingers are the extensions of a verdant heart. A good garden cannot be made by somebody who has not developed the capacity to know and love growing things.

—RUSSELL PAGE, *The Education of a Gardener*

He plants trees to benefit another generation.

—Caecilius Statius

The word humility (also human) is derived from the Latin humus, meaning "the soil." Perhaps this is not simply because it entails stooping and returning to earthly origins, but also because, as we are rooted in this earth of everyday life, we find in it all the vitality and fertility unnoticed by people who merely tramp on across the surface, drawn by distant landscapes.

—Piero Ferrucci

Grow what you love. The love will keep it growing.

—Emilie Barnes

Believe in yourself, your neighbors, your work, your ultimate attainment of more complete happiness. It is only the farmer who faithfully plants seeds in the Spring, who reaps a harvest in Autumn.

—B. C. FORBES

No matter where you are you can grow something to eat. Shift your thinking and you'd be surprised at the places your food can be grown! Window sill, fire escape and rooftop gardens have the same potential to provide impressive harvests as backyard gardens, greenhouses and community spaces.

—GREG PETERSON,
Grow Wherever You Go!
Discovering the Place
Where Your Garden Lives

Why try to explain miracles to your kids when you can just have them plant a garden?

—ROBERT BRAULT

I know the pleasure of pulling up root vegetables. They are solvable mysteries.

—NOVELLA CARPENTER,
*Farm City: The Education
of an Urban Farmer*

When I see that first, minuscule, curled, pale green wisp of a sprout poking up between a couple of grains of vermiculite, I hear God speaking.

—JUNE SANTON

No ray of sunlight is ever lost, but the green it wakes into existence needs time to sprout, and it is not always granted to the sower to live to see the harvest. All work that is worth anything is done in faith.

—ALBERT SCHWEITZER

I cannot rid the entire world of noxious problems, but I can patiently cultivate the good earth around my own two feet and grow what I wish to see in my own back yard.

—JACOB NORDBY

The greatest change we need to make is from consumption to production, even if on a small scale, in our own gardens. If only 10% of us do this, there is enough for everyone.

—BILL MOLLISON

When we grow our food, we participate more fully in nature's cycles and form a closer bond with Mother Earth. Knowing how to grow your own food allows for a sense of freedom and pride that you can feed and provide for yourself, one of the most basic necessities.

—AUTHOR UNKNOWN

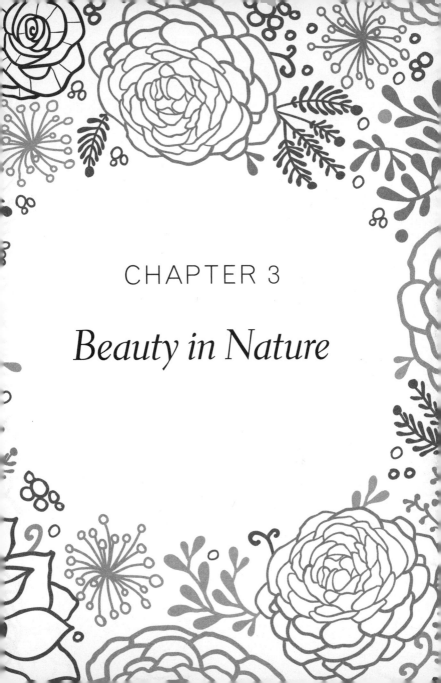

CHAPTER 3

Beauty in Nature

HOSE WHO contemplate the beauty of the earth find reserves of strength that will endure as long as life lasts. There is something infinitely healing in the repeated refrains of nature—the assurance that dawn comes after night, and spring after winter.

—RACHEL CARSON

In all things of nature there is something of the marvelous.

—ARISTOTLE

Nature will bear the closest inspection. She invites us to lay our eye level with her smallest leaf, and take an insect view of its plain.

—HENRY DAVID THOREAU

Beauty surrounds us, but usually we need
to be walking in a garden to know it.

—RUMI

NATURE is what we see,
The Hill, the Afternoon–
Squirrel, Eclipse, the Bumble-bee,
Nay–Nature is Heaven.
Nature is what we hear,
The Bobolink, the Sea–
Thunder, the Cricket–
Nay,–Nature is Harmony.

Nature is what we know
But have no art to say,
So impotent our wisdom is
To Her simplicity.

—EMILY DICKENSON

There is new life in the soil for every man. There is healing in the trees for tired minds and for our overburdened spirits, there is strength in the hills, if only we will lift up our eyes. Remember that nature is your great restorer.

—CALVIN COOLIDGE

Look deep into nature, and you will understand everything better.

—ALBERT EINSTEIN

Most people don't see the sun, soil, bugs, seeds, plants, moon, water, clouds, and wind the way gardeners do.

—JAMIE JOBB

I sit in my garden, gazing upon a beauty that cannot gaze upon itself. And I find sufficient purpose for my day.

—ROBERT BRAULT

Earth teach me to forget myself
as melted snow forgets its life.
Earth teach me resignation
as the leaves which die in the fall.
Earth teach me courage
as the tree which stands all alone.
Earth teach me regeneration
as the seed which rises in the
   spring.

—WILLIAM ALEXANDER

Anything which grows is always more beautiful to look at than anything which is built.

—LIN YU TANG

As one grows older one should grow more expert at finding beauty in unexpected places, in deserts and even in towns, in ordinary human faces and among wild weeds.

—C. C. VYVYAN

I must go to Nature disarmed of perspective and stretch myself like a large transparent canvas upon her in the hope that, my submission being perfect, the imprint of a beautiful and useful truth would be taken.

—JOHN UPDIKE

Though we travel the world over to find beauty, we must carry it with us or we find it not . . . The difference between landscape and landscape is small, but there is a great difference in beholders. There is nothing so wonderful in any landscape as the necessity of being beautiful under which every landscape lies.

—RALPH WALDO EMERSON

The richness I achieve comes from nature, the source of my inspiration.

—CLAUDE MONET

There is pleasure in the pathless
  woods,
There is a rapture on the lonely
  shore,
There is society, where none
  intrudes,
By the deep sea, and music in its
  roar:
I love not man the less, but Nature
  more,
From these our interviews, in which
  I steal
From all I may be, or have been
  before,
To mingle with the Universe, and
  feel
What I can ne'er express, yet
  cannot all conceal.

—LORD BYRON

There is a way that nature speaks, that land speaks. Most of the time we are simply not patient enough, or quiet enough to pay attention to the story.

—LINDA HOGAN

With beauty before me I walk
With beauty behind me I walk
With beauty above me and about
    me, I walk,
It is finished in beauty
It is finished in beauty.

—NAVAHO NIGHT CHANT

To such an extent does nature delight and abound in variety that among her trees there is not one plant to be found which is exactly like another; and not only among the plants, but among the boughs, the leaves and the fruits, you will not find one which is exactly similar to another.

—LEONARDO DA VINCI

Keep close to Nature's heart...and break clear away, once in a while, and climb a mountain or spend a week in the woods. Wash your spirit clean.

—JOHN MUIR

I went to the woods because I wished to live deliberately, to front only the essential facts of life, and see if I could not learn what it had to teach, and not, when I came to die, discover that I had not lived.

—HENRY DAVID THOREAU

The best remedy for those who are afraid, lonely or unhappy is to go outside, somewhere where they can be quiet, alone with the heavens, nature and God. Because only then does one feel that all is as it should be and that God wishes to see people happy, amidst the simple beauty of nature.

—ANNE FRANK

Nature often holds up a mirror so we can see more clearly the ongoing processes of growth, renewal, and transformation in our lives.

—MARY ANN BRUSSAT

Apprentice yourself to nature. Not a day will pass without her opening a new and wondrous world of experience to learn from and enjoy.

—RICHARD W. LANGER

Have you ever noticed a tree
    standing naked against the sky,
How beautiful it is?
All its branches are outlined, and in
    its nakedness
There is a poem, there is a song.
Every leaf is gone and it is waiting
    for the spring.
When the spring comes, it again
    fills the tree with
The music of many leaves,

Which in due season fall and are
    blown away.
And this is the way of life.

    —KRISHNAMURTI

When you take a flower in your hand and really look at it, it's your world for the moment. I want to give that world to someone else. Most people in the city rush around so, they have no time to look at a flower. I want them to see it whether they want to or not.

    —GEORGIA O'KEEFE

Study nature, love nature, stay close to nature. It will never fail you.

    —FRANK LLOYD WRIGHT

Flowers always make people better, happier, and more helpful: they are sunshine, food and medicine to the soul.

    —LUTHER BURBANK

In the end, there is really nothing more important than taking care of the earth and letting it take care of you.

—CHARLES SCOTT

One touch of nature makes the whole world kin.

—WILLIAM SHAKESPEARE

Nothing in the nature lives for itself
Rivers don't drink their own water
Trees don't eat their own fruit
Sun doesn't give heat for itself
Moon doesn't ever go on honeymoon
Flowers don't spread fragrance for
    themselves
Moral: Living for Others is the Rule
    of Nature

—AUTHOR UNKNOWN

I go to nature to be soothed and healed, and to have my senses put in order.

—John Burroughs

The goal of life is living in agreement with nature.

—Zeno, 335 BCE

You must not know too much or be too precise or scientific about birds and trees and flowers and watercraft; a certain free-margin, and even vagueness—ignorance, credulity—helps your enjoyment of these things.

—Henry David Thoreau

Nature never did betray the heart that loved her.

—Wordsworth

Give me odorous at sunrise a garden of beautiful flowers where I can walk undisturbed.

—WALT WHITMAN

Just living is not enough. One must have sunshine, freedom, and a little flower.

—HANS CHRISTIAN ANDERSEN

The creation of the Landscape-Garden offered to the true Muse the most magnificent of opportunities. Here was, indeed, the fairest field for the display of invention, or imagination, in the endless combining of forms of novel Beauty; the elements which should enter into combination being, at all times, and by a vast superiority, the most glorious which the earth could afford. In the multiform of the tree, and in the multicolor of the flower, he recognized the most direct and the most energetic effort of Nature at physical Beauty. And in the direction or concentration of this effort, or, still more properly, in its adaption to the eyes which were to behold it upon earth, he perceived that he should be employing the best means—laboring to the greatest advantage—in the fulfilment of his destiny as Poet.

—Edgar Allan Poe,
　"The Landscape-Garden"

I think this is what hooks one to gardening: it is the closest one can come to being present at creation.

—Phyllis Theroux

Land, then, is not merely soil; it is a fountain of energy flowing through a circuit of soils, plants, and animals.

—Aldo Leopold,
　A Sand County Almanac

I have discovered that I also live in "creation's dawn." The morning stars still sing together, and the world, not yet half made, becomes more beautiful every day.

—JOHN MUIR

We do not see nature with our eyes, but with our understandings and our hearts.

—WILLIAM HAZLETT

I love to think of nature as an unlimited broadcasting station, through which God speaks to us every hour, if we will only tune in.

—GEORGE WASHINGTON
    CARVER

Nature uses human imagination to lift her work of creation to even higher levels.

—LUIGI PIRANDELLO

CHAPTER 4

Garden Wit

H O W   M E your garden and I shall tell you what you are.

—ALFRED AUSTIN

Gardening requires lots of water—most of it in the form of perspiration.

—LOU ERICKSON

"If" is a word that has humbled many gardeners. But it hasn't made us quit.

—KATHERINE ENDICOTT

The more help a man has in his garden, the less it belongs to him.

—WILLIAM M. DAVIES

Successful gardening is doing what has to be done when it has to be done the way it ought to be done whether you want to do it or not.

—JERRY BAKER

Gardener's Recipe: One part soil, two parts water, and three parts wishful thinking.

—AUTHOR UNKNOWN

Nature does have manure and she does have roots as well as blossoms, and you can't hate the manure and blame the roots for not being blossoms.

—BUCKMINSTER FULLER

You know you are a hard-core gardener if you deadhead flowers in other people's garden.

—SUE CARELESS

When weeding, the best way to make sure you are removing a weed and not a valuable plant is to pull on it. If it comes out of the ground easily, it is a valuable plant.

—AUTHOR UNKNOWN

Advice from a tree: Stand up tall and proud—sink your roots into the earth—enjoy the view. Stand up tall and proud. Sink your roots into the earth. Be content with your natural beauty. Go out on a limb. Drink plenty of water. Remember your roots. Enjoy the view!

—ILAN SHAMIR

An optimistic gardener is one who believes that whatever goes down must come up.

—LESLIE HALL

If you are not killing plants, you are not really stretching yourself as a gardener.

—J. C. RAULSTON

Give a weed an inch and it will take a yard.

—AUTHOR UNKNOWN

They know, they just know where to grow, how to dupe you, and how to camouflage themselves among the perfectly respectable plants, they just know, and therefore, I've concluded weeds *must* have brains.

—DIANNE BENSON, *Dirt*

The great French Marshall Lyautey once asked his gardener to plant a tree. The gardener objected that the tree was slow growing and would not reach maturity for 100 years. The Marshall replied, "In that case, there is not time to lose, plant it this afternoon!

—PRESIDENT
JOHN F. KENNEDY

Gardening is cheaper than therapy and you get tomatoes.

—AUTHOR UNKNOWN

I consider every plant hardy until I have killed it myself.

—SIR PETER SMITHERS

We come from the earth.
We return to the earth.
And in between we garden.

—AUTHOR UNKNOWN

Garden: One of a vast number of free outdoor restaurants operated by charity-minded amateurs in an effort to provide healthful, balanced meals for insects, birds and animals.

—HENRY BEARD
AND ROY MCKIE,
Gardener's Dictionary

If I wanted an easy care garden, I would have planted weeds.

—AUTHOR UNKNOWN

In the spring, at the end of the day, you should smell like dirt.

—MARGARET ATWOOD

What is a weed? A plant whose virtues have never been discovered.

—RALPH WALDO EMERSON

Gardening is a matter of your enthusiasm holding up until your back gets used to it.

—AUTHOR UNKNOWN

One of the healthiest ways to gamble is with a spade and a packet of seeds.

—DAN BENNETT

Flowers are not made by singing "Oh, how beautiful," and sitting in the shade.

—RUDYARD KIPLING

A weed is a plant that has mastered every survival skill except for learning how to grow in rows.

—DOUG LARSON

Never go to a doctor whose office plants have died.

—ERMA BOMBECK

The most serious gardening I do would seem very strange to an onlooker, for it involves hours of walking round in circles, apparently doing nothing.

—HELEN DILLON

What this country needs is dirtier finger-
nails and cleaner minds.

—WILL ROGERS

Whoever said do something right the first
time and you won't have to do it again
never weeded a garden.

—AUTHOR UNKNOWN

Perennials are the ones that grow like
weeds, biennials are the ones that die this
year instead of next, and hardy annuals
are the ones that never come up at all.

—KATHERINE WHITEHORN,
Observations

I appreciate the misunderstanding I have
had with Nature over my perennial border.
I think it is a flower garden; she thinks it
is a meadow lacking grass, and tries to cor-
rect the error.

—SARA STEIN

There's little risk in becoming overly proud of one's garden because gardening by its very nature is humbling. It has a way of keeping you on your knees.

—JOANNE R. BARWICK,
in *Readers Digest*

My rule of green thumb for mulch is to double my initial estimate of bags needed, and add three. Then I'll only be two bags short.

—AUTHOR UNKNOWN

God made rainy days so gardeners could get the housework done.

—AUTHOR UNKNOWN

Growth takes time. Be patient. And while you're waiting, pull a weed.

—EMILIE BARNES

Anybody who wants to rule the world should try to rule a garden first.

—AUTHOR UNKNOWN

A garden is never so good as it will be next year.

—THOMAS COOPER

There are no gardening mistakes, only experiments.

—JANET KILBURN PHILLIPS

I am convinced that weeds are just herbs we've not found a use for yet.

—TRISTAN GYLBERD

The success of my garden is built on the compost of my failures.

—JIMMY TURNER

Gardening is the work of a lifetime: you never finish.

—OSCAR DE LA RENTA

When the going gets tough, the tough get growin'.

—AUTHOR UNKNOWN

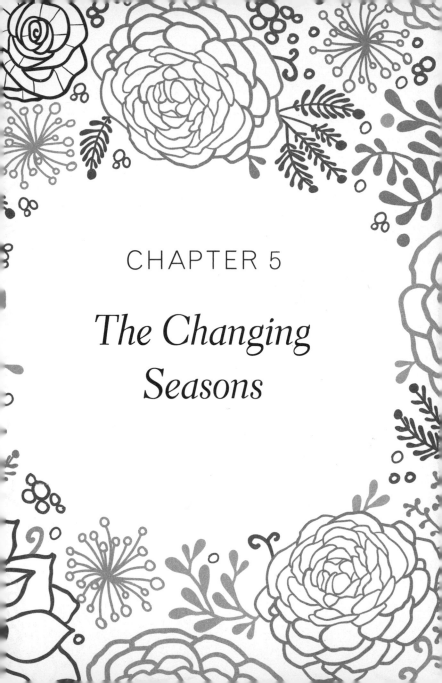

CHAPTER 5

The Changing Seasons

HERE IS no season such
delight can bring,
As summer, autumn, winter
and the spring.

—WILLIAM BROWNE

Four seasons fill the measure of the year;
there are four seasons in the minds of men.

—JOHN KEATS

Live in each season as it passes; breathe
the air, drink the drink, taste the fruit,
and resign yourself to the influences of
each. Let them be your only diet drink and
botanical medicines.

—HENRY DAVID THOREAU

Anyone who thinks gardening begins in the spring and ends in the fall is missing the best part of the whole year; for gardening begins in January with the dream.

—JOSEPHINE NUESE

Gardeners, like everyone else, live second by second and minute by minute. What we see at one particular moment is then and there before us. But there is a second way of seeing. Seeing with the eye of memory, not the eye of our anatomy, calls up days and seasons past and years gone by.

—ALLEN LACY,
The Gardener's Eye

The seasons are what a symphony ought to be: four perfect movements in harmony with each other.

—ARTHUR RUBENSTEIN

At Christmas, I no more desire
    a rose
Than wish a snow in May's
    newfangled mirth;
But like each thing that in season
    grows.

—WILLIAM SHAKESPEARE

January cold and desolate;
February dripping wet;
March wind ranges;
April changes;
Birds sing in tune
To flowers of May,
And sunny June
Brings longest day;
In scorched July
The storm-clouds fly,
Lightning-torn;
August bears corn,
September fruit;
In rough October
Earth must disrobe her;

Stars fall and shoot
In keen November;
And night is long
And cold is strong
In bleak December.

—CHRISTINA GIORGINA
ROSSETTI, *The Months*

Each new season grows from the leftovers of the past. That is the essence of change, and change is the basic law.

—HAL BORLAND

Spring makes its own statement, so loud and clear that the gardener seems to be only one of the instruments, not the composer.

—GEOFFREY B.
CHARLESWORTH

Winter is an etching, spring a watercolor, summer an oil painting and autumn a mosaic of them all.

—Stanley Horowitz

The seasons are what a symphony ought to be: four perfect movements in harmony with each other.

—Arthur Rubenstein

There is a continuity about the garden and an order of succession in the garden year which is deeply pleasing, and in one sense there are no breaks or divisions—seed time flows on to flowering time and harvest time; no sooner is one thing dying than another is coming to life.

—Susan Hill and Rory Stuart, *Reflections from a Garden*

Yesterday the twig was brown
   and bare;
To-day the glint of green is there;
Tomorrow will be leaflets spare;
I know no thing so wondrous fair,
No miracle so strangely rare.
I wonder what will next be there!

    —L. H. BAILEY

Every gardener knows that under the cloak
of winter lies a miracle...a seed waiting to
sprout, a bulb opening to the light, a bud
straining to unfurl. And the anticipation
nurtures our dream.

    —BARBARA WINKLER

In seed time learn, in harvest teach, in
winter enjoy.

    —WILLIAM BLAKE

Have you ever noticed a tree
    standing naked against the sky,
How beautiful it is?
All its branches are outlined, and
    in its nakedness
There is a poem, there is a song.
Every leaf is gone and it is waiting
    for the spring.
When the spring comes, it again
    fills the tree with
The music of many leaves,
Which in due season fall and are
    blown away.
And this is the way of life.

    —KRISHNAMURTI

I've been a dweller on the plains,
have sighed when summer days
    were gone;
No more I'll sigh; for winter here
Hath gladsome gardens of his own.

    —DOROTHY WORDSWORTH

Everything is good in its season.

—ITALIAN PROVERB

But each spring a gardening instinct, sure as the sap rising in the trees, stirs within us. We look about and decide to tame another little bit of ground.

—LEWIS GANTT

All through the long winter, I dream of my garden. On the first day of spring, I dig my fingers deep into the soft earth. I can feel its energy, and my spirits soar.

—HELEN HAYES

There is an appointed time for
    everything.
And there is a time for every event
    under heaven—
A time to give birth, and a time
    to die;

A time to plant and a time to uproot
    what is planted.

    —ECCLESIASTES, 3:1–2

I prefer winter and fall, when you feel
the bone structure of the landscape—the
loneliness of it, the dead feeling of winter.
Something waits beneath it, the whole
story doesn't show.

    —ANDREW WYETH

Just after the death of the flowers,
And before they are buried in snow,
There comes a festival season,
When nature is all aglow—
Aglow with a mystical splendour
That rivals the brightness of spring,
Aglow with a beauty more tender
Than aught which fair summer
    could bring...

    —EMELINE B. SMITH,
      "Indian Summer"

There are two seasonal diversions that can ease the bite of any winter. One is the January thaw. The other is the seed catalogues.

—HAL BORLAND

For the winter is past, the rain is over and gone. The flowers are springing up and the time of the singing of birds has come. Yes, spring is here.

—SONG OF SOLOMON 2:11-12

The day the Lord created hope was probably the same day he created Spring.

—BERN WILLIAMS

Autumn is a second spring when every leaf is a flower.

—ALBERT CAMUS

On this June day the buds in my garden are almost as enchanting as the open flowers. Things in bud bring, in the heat of a

June noontide, the recollection of the love-
liest days of the year—those days of May
when all is suggested, nothing yet fulfilled.

    —FRANCIS KING

Therefore all seasons shall be sweet
    to thee,
Whether the summer clothe the
    general earth
With greenness, or the redbreast
    sit and sing
Betwixt the tufts of snow on the
    bare branch
Of mossy apple-tree, while the nigh
    thatch
Smokes in the sunthaw; whether
    the eve-drops fall,
Heard only in the trances of the
    blast,
Of if the secret ministry of frost
Shall hang them up in silent icicles,
Quietly shining to the quiet moon.

    —SAMUEL TAYLOR COLERIDGE

For man, autumn is a time of harvest, of gathering together. For nature, it is a time of sowing, of scattering abroad.

—EDWIN WAY TEALE

I trust in Nature for the stable laws
Of beauty and utility.
Spring shall plant
And Autumn garner to the end
    of time.

—ROBERT BROWNING

January is the quietest month in the garden... But just because it looks quiet doesn't mean that nothing is happening. The soil, open to the sky, absorbs the pure rainfall while microorganisms convert tilled-under fodder into usable nutrients for the next crop of plants. The feasting earthworms tunnel along, aerating the soil and preparing it to welcome the seeds and bare roots to come.

—ROSALIE MULLER WRIGHT

For lo, the winter is past, the rain
   is over and gone;
The flowers appear on the earth,
   the time of singing has come
and the voice of the turtledove
   is heard in our land.
The fig tree puts forth its figs,
   and the vines are in blossom;
they give forth fragrance.
Arise my love, my fair one,
   and come away.

   —THE SONG OF SOLOMON,
     2:11–13

Learn to be an observer in all seasons.
Every single day, your garden has something new and wonderful to show you.

   —AUTHOR UNKNOWN

That God once loved a garden we
   learn in Holy writ.
And seeing gardens in the Spring
   I well can credit it.

   —WINIFRED MARY LETTS

One of the greatest virtues of gardening is this perpetual renewal of youth and spring, of promise of flower and fruit that can always be read in the open book of the garden, by those with an eye to see, and a mind to understand.

—E.A. BOWLES

I love spring anywhere, but if I could choose I would always greet it in a garden.

—RUTH STOUT

It was such a pleasure to sink one's hands into the warm earth, to feel at one's fingertips the possibilities of the new season.

—KATE MORTON, *The Forgotten Garden*

We cannot stop the winter or the summer from coming. We cannot stop the spring or the fall or make them other than they are. They are gifts from the universe that we cannot refuse. But we can choose what we will contribute to life when each arrives.

—GARY ZUKAV

In the spring, I have counted 136 different kinds of weather inside of 24 hours.

—MARK TWAIN

I love my garden. It is a source of great pleasure and an outlet for creativity. I have always trusted the seasons, perhaps more so than people. Seasons are reliable, a sense of the constant in a chaotic world for me. My world is not so chaotic now-days.

—JANICE KONSTANTINIDIS

In those vernal seasons of the year, when the air is calm and pleasant, it were an injury and sullenness against nature not to go out and see her riches, and partake in her rejoicing with heaven and earth.

—JOHN MILTON

To the attentive eye, each moment of the year has its own beauty, and in the same fields, it beholds, every hour, a picture which was never seen before, and which shall never be seen again.

—RALPH WALDO EMERSON